I0866599

Wilma Wilderness's Guide to... Mushrooms and other Fungi

Written by
Charis Mather

KidHaven
PUBLISHING

Published in 2026 by
KidHaven Publishing, an Imprint of Greenhaven Publishing, LLC
2544 Clinton St., Buffalo, NY 14224

Written by: Charis Mather
Edited by: Rebecca Phillips-Bartlett
Designed by: Amelia Harris

Cataloging-in-Publication Data

Names: Mather, Charis, 1999-.
Title: Mushrooms and other fungi / Charis Mather.
Description: Buffalo, NY : KidHaven Publishing, 2026. | Series: Wilma Wilderness's guide to… | Includes glossary and index.
Identifiers: ISBN 9781534551558 (pbk.) | ISBN 9781534551565 (library bound) | ISBN 9781534551572 (ebook)
Subjects: LCSH: Mushrooms--Juvenile literature. | Mushrooms--Life cycles--Juvenile literature. | Fungi--Juvenile literature.
Classification: LCC QK617.M384 2026 | DDC 579.6--dc23

Printed in China

CPSIA compliance information: Batch #QW26KH: For further information contact Greenhaven Publishing LLC at 1-844-317-7404.

Please visit our website, www.greenhavenpublishing.com.
For a free color catalog of all our high-quality books, call toll free 1-844-317-7404 or fax 1-844-317-7405.

Find us on

All images are courtesy of Shutterstock.com, unless otherwise stated.
Cover – Lauritta, Nikolay 007, Spalnic, grey_and. Recurring – AlinArt, haru_natsu_kobo, Kobee, gomolach, Atelier Mokum, Macrovector. 2–3 – A-photographyy. 4–5 – PRILL, ju_see. 6–7 – Stephan Morris, Charlie Goodall. 8–9 – ressormat, Physics_joe. 10–11 – Hailing L, IgorCheri, Tomasz Czadowski. 12–13 – hsagencia, MakroBetz. 14–15 – badnews86dups, Matauw, N_Design. 16–17 – godi photo, Boris Ipatov, Jaroslav Machacek. 18–19 – MBFotografie, Jaroslav Machacek, NataliSel. 20–21 – PolyakovaN, bonchan. 22–23 – shuttertim82, MISTER DIN.

Contents

Words that look like **this** can be found in the glossary on page 24.

A Wilderness of Wonders

Welcome to Wilma Wilderness's Guide to Mushrooms and Fungi! I am Wilma, and the wilderness is my favorite place to explore. There are so many interesting living things to learn about out in the wild.

There is lots to learn about mushrooms and fungi. This guide covers how they look and where they can be found. It also includes some tips for staying safe when you find them.

Safety warning!!!

Some mushrooms and fungi are **poisonous**. Following the safety tips is extremely important.

Why We Need Mushrooms and Fungi

Fungi are very important to the natural world. When living things die, some fungi help recycle them. This puts healthy nutrients back into the soil and helps plants grow.

Living things that break down dead things are called decomposers.

Fungi are neither plants nor animals. They are their own kind of living thing. Fungi come in many types, including mushrooms and molds. To identify fungi, it helps to know what makes them all different.

Moldy blackberries

Fruiting Bodies

The part of a fungus that grows above ground is called the fruiting body. This part makes spores, which are like tiny seeds. Spores are sometimes stored in flaps called gills under the mushroom cap.

Feature Focus

Here are some questions to ask about fruiting bodies:

What shape is the fruiting body?

What do the gills look like?

Does the fruiting body have a **stalk**?

All Sorts of Appearances

Fungi come in lots of interesting forms.

Blue pinkgill mushrooms stand out because of their bright blue fruiting bodies. Their caps are slightly pointed. These mushrooms are found in New Zealand.

Bearded tooth fungi are also known as lion's mane mushrooms. This kind of fungus grows in a fluffy-looking clump.

Morels look like grey or brown sponges on short stalks. They do not have gills.

Good Places to Grow

Fungi grow out of and feed from a material called substrate. Substrate can include soil, plants, or animals. Inside substrate, fungi make tiny white strands. These strands make up a network called mycelium. Mycelium is the main part of a fungus.

Feature Focus

Asking questions about substrate is an important part of fungus identification.

What is the fungus growing from?

Is the fungus growing from a dead organism or a living one?

Does the substrate look damp?

All Sorts of Substrates

Different kinds of fungi need different kinds of substrate.

Honey mushrooms are parasitic fungi. This means that they grow and feed on certain living things, such as trees. This can cause the trees to die.

Meadow muffin mushrooms grow well in **manure**. They use waste from living things as a source of food.

Mold can often be found on fruit. The mold feeds on the fruit. This causes the fruit to become mushy and rotten.

Staying Safe

It is always important to stay safe out in the wild. It is especially important when around fungi. Some fungi are deadly or **toxic**. Sometimes, even breathing in fungus spores can make people unwell.

Fungi release their spores into the air in different ways.

It is not always easy to tell which fungi are safe and which are dangerous. Many fungi have lookalikes. Lookalikes might look similar, but one kind could be safe and another deadly.

Real chanterelle mushrooms are safe.

False chanterelle mushrooms are not safe.

Safety Warning!!!

Even non-poisonous mushrooms might still be toxic or unsafe.

Poisonous Fungi

These fungi are very poisonous. Stay away from these.

Although they are pretty, fly agaric mushrooms are very dangerous. In the past, this poisonous mushroom was used to kill flies. That is where it gets its name.

The death cap mushroom's name should be a clue that this is a deadly fungus. It is one of the world's most poisonous mushrooms.

When poisonous common earthball fungi are touched, they sometimes break open and release the black spores inside.

Wonderfully Wild Fungi

The basket stinkhorn fungus stands out because of its looks and smell. Its fruiting body is bright red and forms a basket-like shape. It sometimes smells like rotting meat.

Some fungi are bioluminescent, which means they glow in the dark. The fruiting bodies of ghost fungi give off a faint green glow that is easiest to see at night.

Get Exploring!

Now that you know all about fungi and the importance of staying safe in the wilderness, it is time to get exploring. Use this guide to help you as you go.

Take a notebook with you when you go outside. You can write down or draw any interesting fungi that you see. Keep a note of their colors, shapes, and substrates—but remember, do not touch them!

Glossary

cap the top part of a mushroom that often holds spores

identify to find out what something is based on what someone knows about it

manure animal waste, or poo

nutrients natural substances that plants and animals need to grow and stay healthy

organism an individual animal, plant, or other living thing

poisonous dangerous or deadly when eaten or touched

recycle to use again to make something else

stalk the stem, which often supports another part of a plant or fungus

toxic harmful to people, animals, or the world

Index